# young girls

Karenjit Sandhu

Published 2021 by the87press
The 87 Press LTD
87 Stonecot Hill
Sutton
Surrey
SM3 9HJ
www.the87press.com



ISBN: 978-1-8380698-7-2

Design: Stanislava Stoilova [www.sdesign.graphics]

*for young girls everywhere*

# Contents

## 4



## 5



## 6

# 1

## Grey Brown

Her shapely smile means it's time to head to the riverbank. Rituals involving hosiery, apples and bluebells commence. Stained orange georgette. Crepe silk dunked into the mouth of the river; it bleeds. Red brown goulash wrapped in Javanese cloth. A branch from a pine tree is felled and lifted into the sky. Twelve helium balloons. Yesterday's party is done as the sun opens an eye.

## Gossip clings to midriff tops

Gossip had been circulating for weeks about Edith and Aditi and all the goings on that hot Indian summer. Gossip wasn't just lying face up in Screen 2, Aisle E, Seat 3 of the local multiplex cinema, it had leaked across to the bowling alley on Summer Hill. Yes, it was sludgy and tacky as it festered in every hamburger joint across town, but it was pulsing, frenzied and raw. Yes, the stench of it was sickening. Gossip was sweet and overripe, brown. Bruised you might say. Gossip clinging to midriff tops, scalloped edges and crocheted centres, loud and bold and gossiped about. It found its way inside a pair of shoes and flitted all over town fluttering its anecdotal nuggets in and out of Gossip-ready cabs. Climbing through bedroom windows Gossip regaling the time in the photobooth, at the Seven Eleven, in the basement, beside the swings, down the alley, first thing in the morning, last thing at night, looking away, pulsing, frenzied, raw.

## I want to be more provincial

a freshwater rustic
bicycle, I ride
through corn-fed cotton fields
weaving in out, wanting
I say I want
but to want is to desire
to crave and cry out for
a kind of I-can't-live-without-that
or you, or both
wanting and coveting
lies that adulterate on the tip
of my tongue
as I lie here
swallowing the backwater,
petty and blinkered,
setting my heart on it.
What's better than these backwoods
I'm lying in, face up,
dwindling
in the moonlight;
this parish-pump
a jerkwater of provincial life,
lying,
circled, by these girls
draped in chiffon chunnis
hankering

## Daughters tied in rebellious ribbons

washed up
gurning novelty rave act
sharp lines
hectoring

bitter

vagina

axe

bare

faced

brunette

nude

chaos

## Sick

We walked past the fairground in '94 and a woman in a sari,
she gave us a bag of candy floss

a prickly fizz on the tip of my tongue
as I watched her in purple, move

you ate nothing and you said nothing,
apparently you gave up sugar in '92

crowds swallowed you, whole
I belched, and vomited onto my jelly sandals.

## Budapest

I pull into a side road, just before the train station and turn around in my seat to face you. My knee nudges the flask in my cup holder, and it spills all over my thigh forming a little well under the shade of my skirt. I'm embarrassed. But determined not to show it. I sit facing you, staring. Ahead. Your train to the city departs at 8:19. Right now you're stuck at 8:11. You still have tickets to buy. But determined, I will not let you go. Yet. Not until you've said all the things you wanted to say yesterday at dusk. But you were too embarrassed to say it as you passed round burnt meats. Tough. Then unexpectedly you pull your face forwards, our noses touch. And you're looking straight into my eyes, and I'm looking straight into your mouth, and

a thousand yous because you because you than I I grey me pretty you you have a way I into you fleeing this this less dark this

fulfilment grey I you the fleeing you the light and I the long you to belong not you but me and pretty you and grey me flee out

## Sunburnt

She twists my arm
a Chinese burn, she says
searing my skin
burnt, in Zebegeny.
She asks me to stare
into the sun, she says
charing my corneas
burnt, on the river bank
where we lie for hours
on your cotton chunnis
burnt, by the hot pans
you insist on
having with us
as we sunbathe
beside the steaming goulash.

## Shadows in the hazy half-light

a turquoise stone marks the hill town
a palate of blue, green-blue        a silhouette, angular
a hump in the middle of a rouged lip        a sandcastle of soil
a summer house, vacant        a life on the dark side of the mountain
a carafe of rosewater        a maharaja's invitation
a rickshaw waits under        a naked body before a fire
a peacock canopy        a shadow cast, pine trees
a sudden rush of thrills        a lost thought floating
a gust of cold mountain air, hazy, and iffy, and        a cave temple in the distance

## young girls!

Did you make it back
to the reservoir of sadness. Did you watch it
throb and vomit
sugar-coated teardrops
like the ones you'd catch inside striped cones
upside down you'd always turn yours in
to a hat. Cones filled with sweet sobs
heaped residue, high
ready to swap; gloop
stickers,
marbles
hot. Sticky, feigned happiness inside
the corner shop
beside the High Rd in the shadow,
the reservoir.

2

## Prussian Blue

Her collection of chalk means it's time to head to the pavement to chalk up her line of thought. Lilac and yellow stripes. She brings a telescope and they each bring pumpkins. It's June and the TV plays grey reruns. Canned laughter lingers close in the air. There is a discarded pumpkin seed under a park bench. They will care for it by taking turns, planting it in an old school shoe.

## Yours, Guerrilla Fighter

Let me be
your guerrilla fighter
let me count the ways
that I shake you up
you, my milkshake
hues of mint, sugar, ice and cream
you fix your banal into me, my wrists jangle
street saccharine, heaving up
gag sick market fabric.
I wrap you up, your legs and feet
and from No. 4's skip I wrench
a terracotta pot, unloved and chipped
big enough for you; you are the seed
stuck in the gap of Ellora's teeth
I pick you out and heave.
Here, hold this banner; let me be
your cog correction, watch that stamp on your wrist
fade. I wade through that itchy grass
the kind that makes your breathing tight
a green system of blocks of earth
cannon, boat, the sea
and puddles reflecting ploughed fields
imitate the real, let me be
a female torso, yours
up against the wall,
mythical and sloped.

## Her

At your party you rushed around talking to everybody
as I watched from outside,
on the other side of your kitchen window, standing
waiting inside your back yard
burning your books, and remembering Marie LC.

## Hiding in your neighbour's rasoee

The body was found twelve days too late
and when lifted,
crumbled
hot sandstone remains
kept inside Le Parfait jars.
One, three, five
five jars of sandstone
body
lifted to new heights
resting on the rasoee shelf
beside the pickled mangoes
forgotten, sour, winking discontent.
Slowly steamed, liquifying
clams

open

wide

## Jelly's fugitive

Remember from the age of 5 and every year after, your mother hosted these birthday parties for you in your front garden. Long table covered in multiple sheets of green crêpe paper sellotaped together, fading in the sun. We all sat around it our toes grazing the grass. And she would serve us jelly with a big sickly scoop of angel delight. These days it's comforting to think of that jelly. And probably for you, there's much consolation in knowing that you're back with the jelly now. Jelly. Jelly, petrol thickened and smelling of soap. Jelly with its alkali taste, its burnt oils and waste fats. Soap. Remember you liked to watch that soap opera after school on Mondays. The one about a coffeehouse in Hungary somewhere, along the Danube I think. Anyway back to remembering you and the solace you've found in returning to the jelly now, but this time as a flame-thrower tenacious and tacky like treacle. To know you're out there fleeting and fiery in transit, quick to disappear into the exploding jelly clouds. And probably for you, there's much relief in that.

## Sugar in the front seats of cars

we
sit inside
your ca
r

we
wait for
the full m s
o I d
watch a
your sweat be d r i
p

o
n

you
p a ss me a
e a w o suga
t t

I
th nk of w h
you m i g h
s a

y u
d ri v m
o
h e
m

## M.I.A

Standing in a field
outside your farmhouse
at dusk,
I lean against an electric pole –
missing cat
flickering sparks
rain collects
on my bottom lip –
I know you're not
looking for me.

## Sleep

3 months old and wrenched from the carcass of love
restless awake flickering

inside the dark
evergreen

and burnt orange
a bruise on the side of a face

grabbing handfuls
of alfalfa

broomstick lying straight
across a neck

holding up a body
over hind legs

what a treat, they say.

## Postcards and a coke

The spittle in your grin
enough to send me home
but I stayed

it was only right
to thank you for the coke
and the Matisse postcard

the one you stole
from the gift shop
pastel cut-outs, ribbed candy

dank days on the promenade
with you in peacock blue
and all the while, knowing

I skipped summer camp for this.

## Yellowish Ochre

Her penchant for line and colour means it's time to head to the Ecole. So she mutters a quick goodbye to the otters in the Danube. They're bloated and sleepy in the springtime air. Lucien is there to greet her, on time. She's late but filled with these Greek ideas about patterned tights, tennis and the natural form. He pulls out a stick figure, drawn by Matisse he says. She glowers.

## Nude

I am
leaning
leaning
towards
leaning
towards, you
coming closer
to see the tilt
of nude, yours
as I lean
fast
leaning forwards
closer
still
breath, mine
reaches you
lean vertebra
inverse weight
back heels
front toes
lie flat, push
the lean
the slant
nude, yours
slight
spinal flexion
torso, yours
supine grip

release, moving<br>
  further<br>
    clockwise, away<br>
      and lengthen<br>
        lean, stretch<br>
          sacral spine, yours<br>
            flattening out<br>
              posterior ribs, expand<br>
                drawing nude lines<br>
                  earlobe, mine<br>
                    balance hipbone<br>
                      upper thoracic<br>
                        tilted alignment grows<br>
                          shoulder, yours<br>
                            away<br>
                              further<br>
                                stretching scapula, strong<br>
                                  sketch<br>
                                    central axis, mine<br>
                                                          growing apart<br>
                                                            discs compress<br>
                                                              tautening<br>
                                                                collateral ligaments<br>
                                                                  hover unlocking<br>
                                                                    facet joints<br>
                                                                      lumber spine lifts<br>
                                                                        crown, yours<br>
                                                                          ankle, mine<br>
                                                                            nude<br>
                                                                              lines

## On a bus with Paul Cézanne

On the bus route home, he thundered upstairs blotchy and red. Red, and blue on the inside, but not lost. So much fruit, his ripened cherries squished and bleeding, red. Stuffed into his side, back and front pockets of his double-breasted dress coat and trousers of fine wool. He sat in the seat directly in front of me and I could see the back of his neck, yellow. Stripes of orange from the city's August sun. I wanted to say something like, can I give you a bag for your cherries? I thought about opening my mouth, wide, and leaning in to say something like that, but he lifted his fur felt hat, burgundy, and out rolled a stash of cherries onto the top deck. Six rolled beside my feet. I stamped down on each one, quick and hard. Popped, bloody and red. He let out a yelp, blue breath wafted from his mouth, wide. He turned his head and stared at me. Long. Sour. Tacky residue on the soles of my shoes tap, tap, tap.

## Tricks performed at parties for entertainment

Indira yanks it out
Ervin plucks it out
Denise licks it out
Henri drags it out
Ella tempts it out
Sandor jerks it out
Marie charms it out
Rob hurls it out
Louise flips it out
Yusuf woos it out
Edith chucks it out
Lajos bowls it out
Viola talks it out
Endre lugs it out
Aditi jolts it out
          Victor scrapes it
                    out

## Sketching a mouth

You speak lots, of yourself
you forget to stop and ask
her of the things she thinks and all
the matter she might like to speak of
in the aisles of the video shop
or on that night out in town
the music too loud
so when you speak, lots
she can't hear anything anyway.
Your mouth flaps mechanically,
you pucker your lips, occasionally you forget
to ask but then one day you do
on an unusually hot day in April
but first you speak, lots
then you ask what she would like
to do right now –

how about bursting through that high pitched roof?

## Leaving on a full moon

Wolf Moon (10th January) a spillage on the rasoee floor
Snow Moon (9th February) a traffic jam
Worm Moon (9th March) a bout of frosty weather
Pink Moon (7th April) a missing pet
Flower Moon (7th May) a twisted ankle
Strawberry Moon (5th June) a delayed flight
Buck Moon (5th July) a pair of laddered tights
Sturgeon Moon (3rd August) a train missed
Corn Moon (2nd September) a neighbour stops by
Harvest Moon (1st October) a broken alarm clock
Blue Moon (31st October) a stack of emails, urgent
Beaver Moon (30th November) a queue at the magazine stand
Cold Moon (29th December) a phone call, middle of the night

## Who said loving Gauguin would be easy

He brushes past me, his scent
of tarpaulin sits heavy,
saturated, dripping
but strong
like the document folder he carries
under his left arm.
I'm unhappy with what I do next
but I do it to silence all that Tahiti talk.
It's not just that but also for the money,
the French lessons
and all those things Mette told me.
Those angular faces and miserable nudes
fruit totems of fire,
burning,
alight,

heavy
asleep
horse
breast
dead
mountain
orchid
boy
palm tree
mangos
long hair sitting
long back alone
red
skirts tree trunks
patterned bodies
bathing
rituals naked
brown

## Tuesdays we paint with sound

You are intuitively right and that's what counts in the long run. My finger rests on the parrot green, the beginning, and I try to talk to these walls, but they wail back a yellowish brown. Maybe if you and I talk long enough we'll drown out these sonorous walls. One sound at a time. And when they ask us what we're doing we'll say we're performing the biggest steam shovel in history - - -

## Self-portrait

Walking down the parade dressed in yellow flares and a burnt orange hat. Surrounded by this kind of greyness. Walking towards this strange light, to breathe. Pale building, grey facades, walking underneath a pale pink sky. Past a flickering lamppost. A greyed bus station. A vacant coffeehouse. A row of costume shops. Walking beside a window and catching yourself, fleetingly, in a street door. Face reflected, unknown. Vague. What a surprise to see yourself here.

# 4

## Acid Green

Her melancholic stance means it's time to head to the house of a stranger. Crossing the boulevard on tiptoes, she removes her jewels and releases her hair. Gesturing with an enlarged emerald hand to a small cinema where she first met Malcom. The streets are crazed with a lively jade light. Chiffon wafts in the city din and onto the tops of residential rooftops. Look a peacock!

## Din and clang

She begins by looking in the mirror at her torn flesh. Puréed capers visible on her knuckles, darkened by the midnight din. A taste in her mouth – decaying pulse, rotting apple, pop-coloured sin. A distaste clinging. To hands, the walls, and the street outside. Hard-edged fabric of life – telegraph poles, pick-up points and shop fronts da duum da duum da daa. The rattle of freight trains, from outside her window. Inside the heat, restless and claggy. People bustling da duum da duum da daa. Pans clang. Room next door. An elephant. Far far in the future blows its bruised trumpet.

## 15:05

The truck sped off into the distance and my heart sank
it was certain
I was too late to hitch that ride
out
in
to
the grassland with its colony of cuckoos.

Afternoon blazing sun made it hard to look ahead
so I turned back and sat on my haunches
~~breathe~~
forlorn fountain grass
~~hold~~
low-spirited pearl sap
~~release~~
silky tuft pods of glum

I clenched my hand into a fist
and held it up to a passing lynx cat
*take me with you*
I cried
out to those erratic rolling terrains
where the claggy stems gather
in milkweed baths of slop.

Cat reared its head and flashed its teeth,
pointed –
it leapt closer
mouth to mouth
*savanna*
it snarled

it was certain

it sprinted off into the distance and my heart sank
I fell into the road dust and went

*cuck*

*ooo*

*oo*

*ooooo*

the sounds of the city beckoned me back

## Here to burn letters

27th February. Dear, red-hot
plaza on a plinth where rests
a tower made from stacked
wooden crates of brown
birch. 15 feet high. Tower
burns. Inside each crate,
letters. Blazing handwritten
notes. Typewritten words,
burning. Printed
communication, alight.
Lined burning hole punched
burning folded parchment
plain burning scented
burning khadi and handmade
burning scorched edges
crinkled flakes burning down
hemp wrapping shards
burning cotton fabric, printed
burning. Recycled silk
singed orange burning
bonded matt coated
watermarked burning
blackened charred glossed
rag tissue crisped cotton
husk linen burning flax
burning corn burning
mulberry burning seed
burning continues higher:
Entry 4, the *OED*, a burning
letter, written
communication addressed to

a fiery person, raging
organisation, or another
flaming body. Sent by
burning post or messenger.
Burning, ignited letters,
burning yours truly Marie
LC burning tales of the
burning summer of '97
signed Malcom burning
magazine cut-outs with
burning love from Edith
burning polaroids thinking of
you Jamil burning stickers
which burn colours sending
burning kisses, with hugs
Karl xx

## Drinking tectonic tides

The truth is, it's always been about Helene C
her exposed midriff, bare and brown
the brocade blouse I asked to borrow
maybe later, she says.
Oh Helene! I cry that night, drunk
on tectonic tides, high crashing
colours of lilac, gold and mint.
Helene C lives
her half-life in a far corner of the world,
leaning against her favourite lamppost,
outside the metro station
used cigarette in one hand,
chunky bangle in the next.
Adoring corners,
arriving rose-bordered
in her sari, wrapped
twice and then once more,
for luck, she says.

# Kathakali

We met in the dark because there was nowhere new left to meet. I think you removed your sandals; it was hard for me to see. You folded and wrapped your white dhoti over my eyes, carefully. And spun me round for 5, 6, 7, 8. And then some more 9, 10, 12, 15. The instructions were clear. The blindfold must remain. I was to feel my way back to the High Rd and meet you outside the corner shop, fully intact, my hair pinned back at the nape of my neck. Standing in the dark, beside the curb, there was nothing left to feel. So I danced. I remembered the Kathakali from '92 in Sunday school. Subtle yet forceful, left, right, arm left, right leg up and spin low, twist, turn right, left, arm right, left leg up and spin low, twist high, turn, left, right, arm left, right leg up and spin low, twist, turn right, left, arm right, left leg up and spin low, twist high, turn. Repeat. And there I remained, for a day and a half, dancing in the dark, alone.

## Drawing circles on concrete

with pink chalk, in the park
the circular eye descends from the sky – it's evening

late, and the whole circle
of my life scribbled here
we paint over this bright circulous January circle
my birth
quietly circularly pleasurable –
all the other girls, scrunchies and bras,
single-voiced
scribble

victims strapped to this circular bed
circling silence

yet yelling and crying, out
to the pinky circulous night sky –

this moment a clean circularly spectre of my mind, circles of muslin
and circular bones wearing a kiss-me smile

somewhere in the distance, a glass breaks –

we stop

circling

## Modigliani wants you to know this

Most of all, he hates a forced entry.
He leaves his door on the latch, open

wide enough for me to see in
to his kitchen, his table top
covered in the post-it-notes
I shove through his letterbox,
every Monday.

7 months on
and my handwritten notes, still
gravitating towards his doormat –
hallway, covered
lounge, covered
bedroom, covered
ceiling, partially
covered, like his bathroom.

I walk over to the café
across the street from our block

over to his favourite barista
who asks after M, his work.
He no longer paints, oui?
She's concerned:
The last 8 months
no canvas, no brush
almost thirty-five, oui?

I show surprise,
and look up to his apartment.
Really? I say.
Gosh, I hadn't noticed.

## At the preview

I arrive at the museum painted turquoise and dressed as a mermaid, confident, knowing this is what Yoko would want. You tell me that I look ridiculous and what an embarrassment it is to be together at this Cunningham preview, the one you've been awaiting for years. It's what Yoko would want I say, as I adjust my blouse made from an old silk sari, fraying, hollow jade stones, attached with UHU glue. You ask me to wait in the foyer, discretely until the applause. But I won't. I shuffle in with my Kashmiri embroidered tail, undoing, cracked calico scallops, attached with UHU glue. Yes, I am shuffling across this polished white floor, and yes it's distracting, and yes my silk is fraying, and yes my tail is undoing, and yes I am shedding, jade stones and calico shells, and yes they're all looking as I position myself, discretely, beside      Duchamp.

# 5

## Reddish Orange

Her amiable nature means it's time to move out. She leaves the city to forget about isolation, heading south at the service of Victor she will be comfortable. Who could have possibly foreseen this journey to this southern land. A voyage that will certainly echo the indomitable travels of Homer. She raises her glass of pineapple juice and looks forward to the turn of a new century.

## Cape Comorin

I often think of the Cape
            yanking me sideways
into its milky hazy mist

red clay on the beach
            thrusting at Sipi Fair
a no-strings-attached hook-a-duck

moonlit perforations, a disco ball
            spinning in a cave,
wireless speakers dropped

from trees, above our heads
            drifting in the desert heat
constellations go up and down

closer and further, out
            extending sideways
o o t s  o o t s  o o t s  o o t s  o o t s

concrete tubes, scrub and dust
            collapsing into waters, pink
where I wait, headless            and seasick

## My God! What am I doing by the side of this stranger?

A passing body, dressed in white, drops a copy of *Psychology Today* into my lap as I sit, cross legged, in the waiting area. It's the March issue, its back pages a clotted clump. I turn to page 7: *The importance of a social life.* According to Doctor T, a social life must consist of various bonds, not just family, friends and community, but strangers too. I laugh out loud. It's a surprising laugh, one I've not heard before. High pitched and ferocious like a tiger-pistol shrimp catching sight of the pink sun. The waiting area is a 10 x 12 ft room. I walk unafraid to the water dispenser holding the magazine open on pages 7 and 8. I release copious glugs of dispensed water onto this double spread. I let a pool gather. I let it soak, and eventually leak. I walk back to my seat one drip at a time. And as I pass the other waiting bodies, I drop a sodden *Psychology Today* into the lap of a stranger. I return to my original seat. The woman sat to my right shuffles uncomfortably, and the child making shapes on the abacus starts to cry.

## baby

baby couldn't take criticism from Fabri,
you're an unwanted fruit, he said
winking        lugubrious

baby fell in love
with windmills and New Delhi
travelling        unchaperoned

baby went to the market place,
exchanged champagne for a cabbage
munching        prudent

baby, now thirty and unmarried, floated
on the Danube in a black-blue dress
reflecting        innocuous

baby is a sculpture, alive
in the caves of Ajanta
beguiling        fertile

## In the window fast dancing

An apple rots in my bedroom
on my bedside table, icky,
smelling bittersweet. Net curtains
I twitch, observing a telegraph pole
the curve of its cable, I follow
to a tiny bamboo hut, yours
in the branches of a tree.
Your front door, green
I watch [...] climb up
graffiti your hut, Haring style
red yellow purple, green
stick figures palpitate to music
from inside the hut, yours
your multicolour lights are on
rotating, and [...] is in the window
fast dancing. The door opens
and oh it's [...] who climbs down,
petite and attractive, clasping a basket
and [...] is soon followed
by [...] who also grips a basket
but drops it. Dropping a basket of apples
pink yellow red, green, lying
now bruised on the asphalt
below the tiny bamboo hut, yours
lying for months –

caustic

rotting

## Edith, meet me to the left of the coconut tree

the swimming baths of Mumbai / chagrined
our toes / roughly cut tiles / no roses / your
bodice left at the feet of the lifeguard / we
swam / we swallowed / for the drunk and
dreary / the downbeat / arm bands / the enfant
terrible of metropolitan life / the burgers are
cheap / the railway lines are slow / the people
are gelid / the carrots are a luminous yellow /

## Lies

Lie one[1] was hard to stomach because not only did you say that she was in town, but you said that she wanted to see me. On the bus home I thought about your second lie[2] and how it made a strategic reappearance on the opening night of Sipi Fair. I was at my lowest. Indira had set fire to my headpieces and stopped returning my calls. When we met at the coffeehouse, I was ready and waiting for lie three[3]. Biting into a crisp jalebi, I thought back to last summer and your clandestine approach to your fourth lie[4]. Hook, line and sinker, I fell for it. And worst of all I repeated the same lie to Malcolm on his boat moored outside the Ellora cave. You catapult your lies so fast. If I'm not careful I'm in danger of missing a lie altogether, just like I did last week underneath the miscellaneous shelf in the library. Helene stopped by my studio on Sunday. I didn't see her, but she was watching me. She spray-painted lie five[5] on the side of my car. Brutal in silver. Suffering from daytime fatigue, I have come to terms with this fifth lie. The truth is, lie five will never be as bad as lie six[6]. Victor handed it to me on a glossy plate with a side serving of broccoli and purple felt tips. Last night when we were sat on our haunches in the shadow of your porch, I found lie seven[7]. And now I'm shining. Finally dressed in gold. Hat, necklace, dress, bangles and shoes, and I've decided that lie eight[8] will be mine.

---

[1] I've got you into the Kahlo preview next Thursday.
[2] Your goulash is far superior to my mother's.
[3] I've always loved your hair like that.
[4] How on earth did you manage to capture that wry glint in his eye?
[5] I adore what you've done with this place. It fits my own taste exactly.
[6] You have such a knack for picking the sweetest cherries.
[7] Oh wow that colour! It suits you.
[8] Yes, they couldn't get enough of it. The applause – rapturous!

## 16th July, you never made it home

I wanted to say thanks for your (strong nose) valour
when I lost my purse
as we ate your (cherry pout) swiss roll
raspberry, and homemade dhal
in the park on an improvised blanket
for (soft bottom) picnics, impractical
silk. Leaves fell on (frizzy hair) sandwiches, cress
lifted with your grandmother's pickle,
the last to hear the news of your (long neck) earing
in the tall grass, cupid bent.

## Extract from a lecture on the horizontal nude

Let us now turn our attention to form. I would like to consider sculptural form with its horizontal lines and continuous thread. Moving to our next slide you can see an example of a provocative leg. It is evident that any artist's involvement with the Hungarian Association of Women Artists (established in 1908) would have resulted in such an image. The line may indeed be sinuous; however, it is important to note that lying supine represents a careful silence, a form of resistance.

This refers to our earlier discussion on the work of Kathe Kollwitz (1867-1945) and Frida Kahlo (1907-1954), where the nude meets the eye of the viewer, and rather interestingly the brown skinned nude is clothed in a flowery sarong. Let us consider further the sarong and its flowers. These flowers frequently appear in a chrome yellow with a reddish violet reflection. This motif continues a decade later in the work of Georgia O'Keeffe (1887-1986), and of course Amrita Sher-Gil (1913-1941). O'Keeffe and Sher-Gil's nudes refuse to lie on a sumptuous, well-clad, four poster bed. Their nudes are positioned on top of string cots, as seen here on slide 14. In this painting the nude poses a challenge to the forced regality and exquisite splendour which is being celebrated in modernist art at the time. These female painters are championing the output of the Association of Creative Women Artists (established in 1931), which sees the rise of homespun garb draping the brown body of the nude, for example the simple grey cloth. As a result, the four poster bed with its yellow drapery is no more.

Undeniably, artists such as Esmet Rahim (1904-1963) and Erzsebet Schaar (1908-1975) are key in introducing innovative materialities which came to be associated with this "new age" nude. As seen here on slide 19, Rahim and Schaar begin working with handwoven khadi and vegetable dyes. Indigo becomes the colour of rebellion and it is also used in craft disciplines such as Hala pottery. Therefore, returning to the concept of the horizontal nude, it is no surprise that Piroska Futasfalvi Marton (1899-1996) continued to paint the nude as a corpse harnessing an inward gaze. The significance of silence cannot be forgotten here, particularly in light of passivity and submission to the male gaze. These female artists are not excited by the aesthetically alluring, the seductive or the erotic. In contrast to these preconceived notions of the nude as ready, waiting and upright, these artists are reacting against modernism by taking us back to the more vulnerable horizontal axis.

6

## Burnt Sienna

Her knowing look means it's time to move out. She's been here before with no desire to return. The goulash is stale, and the parakeets crisp. Abandoned in the sun for far too long. The clock ticks. 10:42 under the shade of a coconut tree waiting for an almighty drop. Photograph of Zorawar in the palm of her left hand. Photograph of Helen, or maybe Marie, clasped in her right.

## Shimla

When I was about 11, I remember you leaning down over me, from the edge of your chair, as you recounted those tales of Shimla. Your expedition, or pilgrimage I think. To a mandir. In the foothills, past The Mall and the Lakkar Bazaar where you stopped to buy a wooden doll, and then slipped downhill but still made it to one mandir out of ten, in Shimla. White chunnis led you there you said. As you recounted those tales of Shimla. My mind was locked on the soft mohair under my feet capturing my reflection in its ridiculous sheen. And Paris. I was thinking of Paris as you uncased the doll. The one you kept locked in your rosewood box, brown. You said something about how it was mysterious, I think. Harnessing some kind of power, or maybe it was wisdom. No. Maybe it was love, yes, I think it was something like that. But I wasn't in Shimla with you. I was in Paris, alone. South of the Arc de Triomphe. Inside the Musée d'Art Moderne de Paris. Listening to John Cage.

## as I perform a ritual for those who are feeling [dark blue]

as I lay down a blanket for the [tusked] elephants

as I tie a [flowered] veil around my neck [marigold, orange]

as I place an ornament [the shape of a rock dove] on my head

as I paint my hand with henna

as a tiger [near] sits and waits

as I walk past the wall [bitter]

as I step down into the river

as I drop [90] rupee coins and watch them sink [below]

as I pour water [over my body] using a terracotta pot [I stole from K]

as the inside of my mouth turns grey [a feverish cold]

as I clasp the sides of my [transparent yellow] dress [embroidered, dark blue]

as [cream] flowers surround me

as I lie supine

[and drift]

## An invitation to a dinner party

Please arrive
dressed, in a brilliant green
or some kind of flaming red,
Tibetan earrings, hanging
from your lobes
as you sashay
across the Kullu Valley
spritely. Light-footed and delicate
into the arms of Svetoslav, knocking
a turmeric cocktail
staining the white linen, yellow.
Noticing Puss at one end
and you at the other, blinking
wide-eyed glossy-locked
frolicking, in full-bodied coterie
with Kushwant, Helen
and Dewan, 26, and animated
shoulder to shoulder with Roop.
Wanting Roop longingly. It's Kishna Roop
gesturing to Stein and Clive Bell
who's book on 'significant form'
leans in between a carafe and a jar,
in front of paneer from Lahore:
the place where all the artists now live.
Camels, buffaloes
someone mentions an attractive crow
eyeing up the pickled fruits.
Your eyes turn to the seating plan,
a name beside yours. A contemptible name
loathsome offensive and cheap.
You take your seat

clench your teeth
and grin,
politely.

## Inside the sugar factory

So many gaps about why I was there. Why this factory.
Why sugar. Many gaps like this one
          . I was briefly distracted by the dotted trees and all the
          . I looked out of the factory's high windows and
thought
                                        . For miles
and miles, clusters of thatch-roofed mud huts with          and
          .

Pink roses pressed up against          and a white wall. I
listened to the sound of voices,
sonorous and          lifting into          , and I'm not sure why
but the factory sirens began to wail, just in time for          .
I saw          moving. I do remember thinking
          , but I couldn't. A sprawling          . I decided
to          in the grass. I was holding a          and I remember
          , or not. It was vast. But also          , I think.
A palatial estate, or          .
     or     , or          , or          , or          , or
   something else maybe. Why was I          this factory
sugar

## Leaving Saraya

| | | |
|---|---|---|
| (January) | red ochre | there was a strange smell |
| (February) | malachite | the lampshade |
| (March) | copper green | the front cover of a magazine |
| (April) | lapis lazuli | a box of cassettes, unmarked |
| (May) | gold | there was something in the air |
| (June) | burnt umber | like a bloodied hand |
| (July) | brown earth | a mother's brooch |
| (August) | alizarin | pinned to a pair of jeans |
| (September) | pink brick | there was an attitude |
| (October) | indigo | of distrust and a no thank you |
| (November) | zinc white | snub inside, outside |
| (December) | bone black | the mountains brewed |

## /solo

/driving alone in the dead of night. 4 am is good, solo
/deafening orange streetlights refract in the glass ahead
/nowhere feels good, numb
        /one hand on the wheel and another inside a bag
of candy floss
/stuffing an open mouth, one fistful at a time
        /to be sick on the open road, in the dead of night,
the only place to be
/happy, and not thinking

## Framed photographs of foreign places

Found (2021)
*Shimla*, 1924
Calotype [15 x 11 cm]
Framed, teak

Found (2011)
*Lake Balaton*, 1932
Albumen print [10 x 7 cm]
Framed, satinwood

Acquired (2004)
*Benaras*, 1927
Autochrome [12.5 x 6.5 cm]
Unframed

Found (2001)
*École des Beaux Arts*, 1933
Daguerreotype [17.5 x 8.3 cm]
Framed, calamander

Inherited (1998)
*Delhi*, 1937
Carbon print [14 x 7.5 cm]
Framed, rosewood

Endowed (1995)
*Punjab High Court*, 1937
Collodion negative [3.2 x 2.7 cm]
Unframed

Bequeathed (1989)
*Budapest*, 1938
Cyanotype [25 x 21 cm]
Framed, mahogany

## You on top

If I knew the true extent of what you're thinking and feeling every day all day, I would perish. But before my soul puffs, I drown in the deluge of a new real future. The new real chokes my imaginary one. Flinging my bubble gum and kulfi mix into the gutter. Washed up tragedy, well wadded stupidity. Hearing the turf grow above my head. Graved grass, split soil. Heartbeat, a squirrel. Jaunts to an ear. My ear, buried underground. Ba bom. I'm on the other side

---

of silence, resting

## Note on text

The poems in this collection take inspiration from the life of Hungarian-Indian artist Amrita Sher-Gil (1913-1941). Born in Budapest, Sher-Gil went on to study art in Italy and France before making India her home. Sher-Gil's paintings document the various locations and people she encountered throughout her lifetime. Heavily influenced by Post-Impressionism, Sher-Gil's paintings capture human emotion and the female nude. The title of this collection is taken from Sher-Gil's painting *Young Girls* (1932), in which two young women sit side by side in conversation with each other. This collection of poems is a reimaging of Sher-Gil's life as a young girl in the 1990s and 2000s.

## Acknowledgements

This collection would not have been possible without the support from the87press. Eternal thanks to Azad Ashim Sharma and Kashif Sharma-Patel for believing in this project, and for being there every step of the way. Thank you for all your phone calls, pep talks and advice. Thank you Kashif for your editorial vision.

I am grateful to Yashodhara Dalmia for *Amrita Sher-Gil: A Life* (Penguin Books, 2013). This book has been an invaluable resource helping me piece together Sher-Gil's history and artistic practice. Thank you for a rich and meticulously researched biography.

Thank you to my teachers at Royal Holloway, University of London, with special thanks to Robert, Dell, Will, Adam, Prue and Eley. And thank you to all the friends I have been lucky enough to meet along the way: Nadira, Tiff, Sarah, Astra, Mae, Caroline, Briony and Cat. And thank you Ryan, Nisha and Sejal for being there right from the beginning. A special thanks to Ryan for your careful and inspiring feedback on many of the poems in this collection.

A big thank you to my family - Mum, Dada, Shimbi and Harvey – thank you for your unwavering love and reassurance. And thank you to Chris for every single conversation. Couldn't do this without you.